T

BIBLE

By: David Bravo Jr.

For my family. Past, present, and future.

Thank you for inspiring me.

Introduction

Disclaimer ☺

Introduction

I've been in the title insurance industry for 17 years, 14 of which were as an account executive in the challenging county of Los Angeles. I was fortunate to work with some of the absolute best title representatives around throughout my career. Los Angeles is a competitive market that will humble you very quickly if you do not apply yourself every day. More importantly, I watched and learned how top reps got to the top and why they stood there. I was tired of being a student and I committed to my absolute full potential in 2007 during the first glimpses of the "great recession". Life changing events and commitments allowed me to make more money during the recession, than in ANY booming market. I realized it's not the market; it's me and my mindset! My mindset and it's execution, is what allowed me to reach the upper echelon of all sales reps and receive national recognition for the years to follow. My life was blossoming while the world was crumbling, I say this with a certain humbleness and awareness, because not everyone has the ability to make the money you could potentially make. Not everyone has the freedom to be the best and get paid for it. Do not let this opportunity slip through your hands just because you are satisfied with mediocrity! I applied every chapter of this book and I hold no secrets back. I'm now a sales manager for a large successful title company in Los Angeles. While writing this book, I asked myself "Why give away all your secrets to the competition?" The answer is, I have no fear of building up the competition because anyone that is willing to work hard and open their mind to being the best deserves every opportunity to succeed! It's not about me anymore (or even my competition), it's about raising the standard of our title and escrow industry across the country. Here's the kicker.....many of you will read this book and say it has good stuff and great ideas but never apply any of its strategies! BUT some of you will read this book and commit yourself to the best career in the world.........see you at the top!!

Disclaimer

Writing this book has been no less than a three year journey for me. When I became a sales manager, I often said there really should be a training manual for getting into the business. Anyone I have ever spoke to in title was basically given a box of business cards and told to go talk to agents. That's about it. So I began writing this book chapter by chapter on my telephone with my thumbs many times in my car, while something came to me from a real life experience. After I finished a chapter, I would just email myself to save it. I throw this caveat out there because I am the author and only editor of this book. So if you find some punctuation or grammatical errors, I'm sorry. I also apologize if some of the verbiage is in any way offensive, I wrote this book with extreme passion for the subject matter. Last but not least comes the ever so omnipresent CFPB and governing bills such as California's SB133. Please check with any and all regulations or restrictions before attempting to implement any activities outlined in the book so you don't get your hand slapped! That's all, enjoy!

Chapter 1   What is your

WHY?

What is your **Why**? A Why is the reason *why* you are going to succeed by out smarting, out lasting, and out working your competition. Why are you going to commit your heart and soul into being the best sales person you can be. A Why is quite simply your motivation. If you don't have a strong enough Why, please stop reading this book immediately and mail to.....for a full refund because the rest of the chapters will be worthless! It's amazing to see what will push and drive anyone to success. It can be your family. It can be your children or spouse. It can be the dream house, car, or money itself. It can be to pull you from poverty. It can be greed. It can be simply the addiction to competing at the highest level. It can be the **vanity** of being on top, from the wise words of Al Pacino "...my favorite sin." The reason behind the Why is irrelevant, but required. Your Why is what is going to wake you up at 6:30am every day to get out to a local coffee shop in your territory so you can send out thank you emails and cards from yesterday's production. As your first stop begins at 8:30 with the top producing early birds beginning a relentless planned attack on potential customers, while maintaining an already thriving book of business. For the next 10 hours your day will be a strategic arsenal of business strategies of success. **This isn't checkers, its chess!** Forget a sit down lunch at a local diner; just be happy you had enough time to go drive thru at In N Out! And if you're really lucky, maybe a 3pm drive thru Starbucks to ramp up the 4th quarter of your day. When you get home, you will look back on your work day and be grateful it will begin again in only 12 hours. As you lay in bed, you get anxious of the next day because you know you're only a few hours away from #Beastmode once again. This is the power of your Why, it pierces your soul with so much force this day is your norm. I promise No Why, No success. This I know with absolute certainty.

Now you might be asking yourself "What is my Why?" and sometimes the answer might not be as black and white as you'd like it to be. This is a great opportunity to set some goals for yourself right now! Look deep inside yourself and if you only had a decade left on this earth and you can do anything, be anything, go anywhere, what would you do!?!? Commit yourself to something! The answer is irrelevant, *how* the answer effects your life on a daily basis is important. If you do not have something that will swift kick you in the butt right now, then DREAM BIGGER. I remember talking to an agent once about what his dreams were. He was a strong man of faith, and he said "One day, I want to have enough money in the bank to start a nonprofit foundation to get Jesus Christ's word out to the youth." What an absolutely incredible Why! Not too far away from this agent, I spoke with another successful agent, but this guy was only 20 years old. I asked him why he prospected every day and worked so hard. His response to me was "David, I honestly want to buy a home as soon as possible, so I can get as many hot girls as I can get......." I won't finish the statement for a variety of reasons. Here we have polar opposites of the reason for working your butt off. One man who wants to give to the community and another who wants pretty women. I love these polarizing viewpoints of how differently someone's Why can be. The actual Why is irrelevant, the real question is will this Why burn into your heart so bad that nothing will come in the way of you and your success! Now I'm not naive enough to think greed, money, fame, and notoriety doesn't drive some people to the top. I am also not naive enough to know that with enough money in the right person's hands, she can make a positive difference in the world. Whatever your Why is, I dare you to get pictures of it and put them in your car visor to look down at you every day. I want you to feel GUILTY for going home at 4pm. I want you to pass by various real estate offices and lenders embarrassed to look their way because YOU know there is business there, that you are not going to get because you want to be home on your old couch looking at your uneventful Facebook feed. Just realize that the top guy or gal in your area is going to make sure you never have the income they have. Need some more guilt and want an easy Why? While you're watching Dr. Oz or ESPNews in the middle of the day. I hope you know there is an office full of hard working people who not only were to the office by 8:30, but who will stay until after 5. These people have families who depend on their livelihood of earning a paycheck every month. They do not have the freedom to make hundreds of thousands of dollars. They instead rely on **YOU** to bring in the biz. You need to wake up, get customers, keep customers, grow your business, work harder than the competition, and do not stop working for the day until you have surpassed your daily goal!! If you cannot do this effectively, people will lose jobs. That's the truth, if a company has no sales, there is no receptionist, no customer service, no title officers, no escrow officers, and there is no company. That's Why.

As I began 2007, it was all fun and games. I had a solid career as a title insurance sales rep, just bought an 825k home a couple of years prior. I had a son and got the chance to marry my eventual "backbone" wife. I just closed escrow on a high rise condo in Vegas and even opened a side hobby business which I gladly invested 150k cash into because why not? Money was easy. THEN, I will save the *woe is me* story over the next year but fast forward to the end of 2008. As I moved my wife and son into my mother Socorro's house, my Why was so harsh it was **beautiful**. Does this story sound familiar to anyone? It's interesting because before 2008 I had never had a Why, I was successful not because of me but because I was a derivative of the abundant real estate market. The mid 2000s were the worst markets in the world for anyone in title or escrow because it was sooooooo easy! I don't care if you were never in the business and worked half days, the market was going to support you. It was going to make you think huge success can come without true ground 'n pound! Spring of 2007, we were a sitting surfer waiting for a little set not noticing the tidal wave approaching!

So back to my Why, I finally had one in 2008! My Why was to never put my family thru a family financial collapse ever again and get back on my feet as quickly as possible. My Why was to beat the market. My Why was to create something that my wife and kids could be proud of one day! Over the next few years, I realized the greatest self-potential of my career. I was able to commit my mind body and soul in 2009 and pay off 75k of debt. In 2010, I was able to purchase a home. In 2011, I made the most money ever in my career only to be eclipsed by more money in 2012. My family grew with more children, forcing a purchase of our dream home the same year. 2011 and 2012 allowed me to be recognized nationally in the highest echelon of title sales reps for the largest title company in the nation. I have to repeat this because you need to get this.......I made more money in the GREAT RECESSION than in any real estate boom. To be clear, this was not my intention. My intention was to relentlessly offer honest superior service to my customers and I was not to be stopped. My success and income was empirical evidence it is not the market. You must know this, your success or failure is not the market! A strong enough Why will push through ANY market. I had a Why that kept me up until 2am some nights with butterflies and I plotted my next day of work. Does your Why do the same? It has to if you want to compete at the highest level! If you aren't ready to commit to your Why, this book isn't for you....

Chapter 2   Appearance of

Success

For many of you, this Chapter is going to cover many basic standards of business that you might feel not required to implement due to having some longevity in the business. To the veterans who read this with a smirk and say to themselves "that's great......for a rookie" I ask you, when was the last time you received an annual award only given to the top reps of your company? And would you have still received this award if you were at a the best local company with the best competition?

First and foremost, dress code needs to be addressed. Men and women, do you wear a suit? Men, do you wear a tie? Men, are your shoes shined? Women, is your hair and makeup appropriate? Men, are you clean shaven or maintain a well groomed beard or mustache? **Do you always wear your name badge?** And finally, do you adhere to these standards every day including Friday? I remember watching a classic interview by Deion

Sanders, in which he spoke of his own personal standards of dress while in the NFL. He directly attributed some of his success to "When you look good, you feel good. When you feel good, you practice good. When you practice good, you play good. When you play good...you eat good."

I cannot stress this basic requirement enough, and I would love to have you think long and hard about your attire. When you are wearing your best outfit possible, the one that fits just right, don't you feel good? When you leave your home looking like a million bucks, aren't you telling yourself "I can't wait to see my favorite accounts and get in front of new customers today!" This initial commitment to look your best has already altered your state of mind. The mental warfare on ourselves (men) begins with putting a dimple in your Ike Behar necktie because you know at least 5 people are going to compliment that knot!

Women, when you are wearing a brooch so beautiful that you know it's going to be hard for your clients NOT to compliment it because it makes your suit look gorgeous. **The biggest question is can you commit to this every day, including the personally HATED casual Friday?** If you can do this every day, this is a HUGE start to your amazing day. The biggest challenge you will face is not having enough A+ outfits, but can at least you can commit to keep wearing them. Every paycheck, you need to start investing in a beautiful blouse, a thick bold neck tie, a shirt with French Cuffs that presses well, shoes that shine, or a sophisticated skirt that will have them asking where do you shop. What we put on in the morning will dictate the success of your day, without fail. This I know for a fact because I dare you to try to ask for business in a wrinkled tee shirt for a month and watch what happens to your business! The rule still applies, now watch what happens when you dress classy and sharp every single day! When I'm wearing my best shirt, best tie, and best shoes….I GUARANTEE you I'm about to have the best day of my week!

Some other notable basics are wash your car weekly, always keep a small stack of unbent business cards, and always have a smile :) I'm big on washing my car after an event in 2008. Just after one of my good customer's office meeting that was held off site, the broker was walking with me talking business. As we approached the parking lot, the broker asked me "Hey Jr, can you give me a ride back to the office? I came with my wife but she had an appointment." To which I instantly replied "Of Course". As the words left my mouth, I realized I just had a drive-thru lunch and a car full of scattered flyers, water bottles, and plenty of miscellaneous trash scattered throughout. The only thing I remember was one of my top brokers entering the car saying "Wow, you really don't take care of your car do you." Absolutely embarrassing and I hope it never happens to you! By the way, always keep a pack (or 3) of fresh seated gum in your car and disposal dental floss sticks. From the wise words of my father **"there is nothing worse than a salesperson with bad breath".**

I cannot stress enough how much these little things can affect your business. If you cannot do the little things perfect in your life, how can you be expected to come through with perfection on the big things? It almost can be a little OCD at times but you need to be ready and prepared for a successful day, every day! This all goes back to your Why! Hopefully there is a little part of your Why that includes looking and feeling good. When you surround yourself and your actual body with higher standards of success, you will create a mindset that will require nothing less but a great work day.

And to finally caveat this chapter's dress code, you might be reading this under the Texas summer sun saying, no one wears what he is referring to during these months. I'm fully aware of territorial and weather conflicts when dealing with dressing up every day, you need at least be the best dressed for what your territory and weather deems necessary! Even if you work in Honolulu, and Hawaiian shirts are the norm for business....then you better wear the BEST Hawaiian shirt possible in front of customers. At the end of the day, be the best dressed title rep in your territory and be the best representation of yourself wherever you work or whatever month it is. <u>Raise your daily appearance standard for work IF you want to raise your personal standard of living.</u>

Success

It may be tough for many of you to set up a solid schedule because you are new. So who do you target? How do you target? And why are you targeting them? This is where information is power, the key is...how we get a hold of it. Many states and markets offer "market watch" programs that will email you your area activity. This activity is whenever a listing is taken/becomes pending/and sold. Some of these programs will give you complete agent information including office, email, and even phone number. Through these reports, you could even run general lists like the top 200 listing or selling agents. This is **GOLD** because if you want title and escrow, you know to specifically target these top agents doing 80 percent of the business. If you are in home warranty or work for a termite company, run the top selling agents! They are your yellow tail tuna pod in the middle of the Pacific Ocean! Please Google MTA or REA reports to see what I'm talking about.

If you don't have systems like these to make you prospects info sent to you, don't worry because your competition doesn't either and the playing field is even. The process of finding customers is the same as it always has been. Join the Board, research new offices and GET ROSTERS (more later)! Organize these accounts into ABC levels. The A offices, or even individual clients, are the absolute cream of the crop in the industry. Rain makers that will let you buy your dream home or Tesla Model S. These offices will many times have existing relationships (more later). The B customers are rock solid offices that will do the consistent volume to feed and take care of your family. The C customers are where you will be able to pick off the lower hanging fruit and get your order count going. Chances are they do not have strong existing relationships and can be won of with basic early consistency. Just to be clear from the wise words of Joe V "**You were not born to be AVERAGE**" so if your aim is to be the best rep in your area, working with the best agents, and offering the best service.... why would you want to work with the average C offices. I'm not saying that an average office can't have some great agents, that's different because we now focus on those specific agents. I am saying an average small office with average small producing agents shot NOT be your end game. They key is this, no matter who you are working with right this moment, the eventual goal is to fill your customer list with A and B offices. There is no other way to get to the top. It is impossible to get to the top working with agents who do one deal per quarter. Now no one said it was going to be easy, and this is definitely something that will not happen in a couple of weeks or even month. This will take over a year minimum, just to get the ball rolling. They key is you need to have the mindset "if I plan on being a rep for any amount of time, longer than a couple of years.... I might as well structure my business plan to work towards eventually working with the best! ". Even if you are not working with the best yet, at least set your eyes on the prize.

Chapter 4   Schedule your

Success

Any successful salesperson, in any field, has a schedule. The details of the schedule will dictate the levels of success. There are certain daily activities that need to happen without compromise. You need to be dressed and out in "the field" by 8 am, unless you have taking the kids to school commitments. Your schedule should begin with getting to a certain spot (or rotation of spots) which you can also send early follow ups, emails to potential customers, thank you cards for yesterday's business, or prepare promotional items for the day. This first step is crucial to have in place as a habitual event. It sets the tone for the day. Now let's get into every day separated from each other. At the minimum, buy yourself a dry erase board separated into days of the week. **Each day should list your scheduled stops of either A, B, or C offices and customers.** I would even recommend you list every office in your area and attribute their number of transactions next to them….whether you work with them or not. This is an important eye opener because it starts turning business into math! Start to see the potential of what your day or week should look like, along with the potential transactions per week looks like as well! Something simple like this……

OFFICES I'M NOT CALLING ON	# OF MONTHLY DEALS
C21 Goldmine	30
Remax Bigtime	25
KW Kiss Me	25
C21 Happy	30
Brookshire Hathaway	20
Real Estate Smile	20
ERA Heaven	25
Mom and Pop	10
Mom and Pop	15
Blue RE	10
Red RE	5
ETC	5
ETC	10
ETC	15
ETC	10
ETC	5

Now that you have your core customers and prospects, incorporate your customers and fill that schedule. **Huge tip....your days should be strictly based upon when your customer office meetings are.** It is imperative that you start going to every office meeting possible, every week. Office meetings are when and where you will find the realtors! <u>This is when and where you have to show up! These meetings are where you will make your most contacts possible in one day!</u> Boiler Room style "it's a contact sport, the more contacts you make the better you'll do".

In addition to office meetings, you have to attend monthly Board of Realtors meeting. Pay the affiliate dues with a smile and be there! There are NO closed offices at board meetings. Once again, this is where contacts will be made. Not only will you be given the opportunity to see your existing clients in your area, but these meeting are a petrie dish for growing new business. The glory of being a fixture on the wall of office and Board meetings are the eventual opportunities to get to speak at these events. Finally your "dog and pony show" gets to be heard! I don't care what is said when it's your turn up to bat but you have two options, make it informative or make them smile. Give them market sales stats or tell a joke, that's it. Agents want data like sales prices, foreclosure stats, # of home sales, and or even scenarios they should avoid with their escrows. They don't care about your experience and do not tell them how you'll work hard for them, be quiet and let your hard work say that! Later on you can sprinkle in new company products, but only after you have proven yourself as the market expert.

A summary of an office visit schedule is, based around (1) office meeting, (2) board meetings, (3) current top offices serviced (4) top prospects (5) escrows, if your market has independents or are not an actual escrow rep (6) current other offices serviced.

Make Every Day Count

MON	C21 Sky, KW City, Remax Net, Realty World. ERA Town, C21 Home, New Office, New Office 2
TUES	C21 Street, KW World, Mom and Pop1, Mom and Pop2, C21 Sky, Remax Home, HomeSmart
WED	Brookshire Hathaway, USA realty, Mom and Pop 3, Remax Net, First Team RE, KW City
THUR	Board meeting, Remax 1, Coldwell Banker A+ Ebby Halliday RE, West RE, Mom and Pop 4
FRI	KW City, C21 SKY, Remax 3, Realty World, Number 1 Realty , Mom and Pop 5, RE Town
SAT	Open Houses, Top Real Estate Office you have, other Top Real Estate Office you have

Again, I cannot stress enough every scheduled day must be worked around where you are going to see the most customers. Schedule your days and routes strictly based around where your offices meetings are. The closer proximity your office schedule looks like, the more efficient your day is! **SCHEDULE SCHEDULE SCHEDULE!** If you fail to plan then you plan to fail! This is true about any person of business. I have sat with so many sales people and began with the fundamental question "Can you please tell me your schedule?" I guarantee their schedule will directly correlate with how much (or lack of) success they are experiencing. This isn't some higher form of selling, it's fundamental to its core and must be done if you want to get to achieve higher levels of success.

Chapter 5 Create Relationships

(Open Offices)

It's time to have some meat and potatoes, maybe even a can of corn. It's time to go get it! We know our plan, we are dressed for success (with a badge), we know our territory, and we know our goals and objectives, now it's time to make our calls. One of the things that I found was helpful while driving to my territory or even between offices, was getting either some music on that fires you up or play a motivational audiobook that got me motivated. For most of 2013, I would loop Eric Thomas' motivational Mix Tape over, and over, and over. I dare you to let him pierce your soul! You should be bouncing out of the car with a huge smile and a hop in your step every day, and on every call. So let's go! On a cold call....... As soon as you open the door, the first person you make eye contact with you should be saying "Hi how are you". If it is the front desk person, give a warm introduction by saying "Pleasure to meet you, my name is (first and last) and I work with (your company aka the greatest company in the world). I am the preferred rep who will be servicing your office. Before I visit the agents, is there anything you need up front? Pens or scratch pads?....... Thank you so much." <u>Smooze the gate keeper! This is so important to do, every time every day, on every stop.</u> This person who is behind the front desk will hold the first opportunity to your success and they must be worshipped accordingly. If this person says "Nice to meet you, come on in" you are golden! Chances are you have just encountered an OPEN OFFICE.

Ask them where the broker or manger sits so you can introduce yourself the same way you did earlier and proceed. This time follow up the smile introduction with additional service orientated value "Thank you Mr(s). Manager/Broker for allowing me to be of service. I will be calling on your office weekly. Is there anything specific that I can contribute to your agents that you find to be of importance to your team. Monthly market data, education, trainings?" What you just did was open the door to being of service to not only the eventual agents who give you deals BUT you are positioning yourself as a teammate to the broker/manager and a possible checkmate later. While they are answering you, smile and quickly scan their desk immediately to find ANYTHING in common. "Oh you also have a son in little league, what park does he play at? What year did you graduate from Notre Dame...my cousin went there? Oh you like the Yankees, that's awesome... Jeter was really one of the best ever (I hate the Yankees but I love success) "Oh you have a beautiful purse, have you seen the new line from Coach? Oh wow, you went to the Mike Ferry Superstar Retreat? I was there too! What did you think? Wasn't it awesome?" Close with....."Here's my card, look forward to being of service :) ". It doesn't matter what you ask, it is developing rapport! After a brief conversation, continue on to the agents and follow the same steps. "Hi my name is......anything I can get you today to make your life easier? (MY ABSOLUTE FAVORITE QUESTION, more later) Hey I also have an English Bulldog, aren't they the best? Here's my card, see you again soon :) ". Remember to develop rapport and continue this script on every agent and SMILE! As you work your way through the office, continue working your way to the processors or coordinators. Treat the processors the same way you would an agent! Many times the agents let them open the order with whomever they want. As you finally make your way to leave the office, stop by the manager/brokers office to say thank you again! Let them know they have a great team! Finally say thank you (again) to front desk. By the time you reach your car, you need to activate you memory bank or take notes. Seriously, take notes if you have to. The information gathered must be brought up again the next time you see them to continue the conversation. This is imperative!

Next time you see Joe Agent ask "How was little Billy's ball game over the weekend did they win?" What you're really telling them is they are important to you, they matter, and they need to give you their next deal because you care! And do yourself a favor and actually care. For the agents that are not in the office that day, here's a huge tip..... Leave your business cards either on their phone or on the keyboard. This forces them to pick up your card! As you continue to call on this OPEN OFFICE, you are going to find yourself running out of things to say because "Hey need a property profile?" gets old! I go back to my open all-time favorite line "How can I make your life easier?" It's opened ended, and demands an answer other than no. You will also find the occasional funny response like "Ya, a million dollars" back at which point you buy a pack of fake jumbo million dollar bills and staple your business card to one, leaving it on their desk.

Back to that cold call, lets change the scenario and after your smiling hop step introduction, the front desk person (or anyone for that matter) says "I'm sorry we are a CLOSED OFFICE". This is probably a common occurrence to a good office, and you need to be sure the next words out of your mouth are prepared. "That's awesome, there is a good chance I will still be servicing the office since work with many other professionals in the area. Are there any supplies, pens, desk calendars I can get for you? (you should just give her pens or highlighters at that point if you have any with you) Thank you Sarah, it was a pleasure to meet you. Here's my card, can I have your brokers/managers card? :) ". Based upon your research this will be an office you have to do more reconnaissance on, and attack a completely different way. Let's do it, it's about time we have some fun!

Chapter 6   Closed Offices,

My Fav

So many of you probably read the last chapter and we're saying "Ya right! It's not that easy! I can't just walk right into a top office and solicit business, they won't even let me passed the door!" and your probably right! The difference between the top rep in your area and you is simple; the top rep somehow obtained access to these offices at one point which propelled him to the top! Now it's your turn. So as you walked up to the wonderful front desk person the script goes a little something like this "Hi pleasure to meet you, my name is_____ with (the best title company ever) and I will be servicing this territory. Before I meet the agents, do you need anything up front? Pens? Desk calendars?" They respond "Actually we're not a closed office and we don't let other reps go back there" at which point you should respond "Sorry to hear that, either way do you still need any supplies up front? (hand over pens regardless of their answer) Can I have the broker's or manager's business card, I would still like introduce myself." Take the business card and your intro email should probably read....... Hello Mr(s) Broker Manager, my name is_____with_____. I stopped by your office earlier and wanted to introduce myself. I look forward to one day meeting you in person, I have heard nothing but great things about you and your operation. Please let me know how I can be of service or make your life easier! ". That's it, short a sweet and especially DISARMING! Most importantly, your seed officially has been planted. Make sure you also send a thank you card to the person up front, disarm them immediately as well because you WILL start working with that office and **you need them on your side.** As you leave the top producing office, this is where the fun starts.

You need to start "Pinging" the agents of the office "Congrats on your new listing on_____" and start soft selling every agent there (I will cover this next chapter). The hardest part of getting into a closed office is getting yourself to work with ONE agent. That's all you need is ONE! Once you have one agent, you now have a reason to stop by the office and more importantly get to where the agents are to meet your ONE customer. Coincidentally you are going to say hi to everyone else, but how do we get that one? Start pinging! I don't care how much control an office manager or broker has over their people, I guarantee there is a weak one in the bunch or even a rebel new agent looking to give an outsider a try! Start pinging! Once you get one, it's over! Now let's say you've been pinging for months and you haven't received an opportunity from anyone. What do we do? Welcome to NDC......

I wish I can take credit for NDC but I can't, thanks Ron for the Darrel Turner paradigm shift of 2007. NDC stands for Non Directing Customer. NDC is a strategy used by a sales rep to get new customers. In any real estate transaction, most of the time you will have a different selling agent than the listing agent. It doesn't matter who got you the deal, one of them specifically didn't choose you or even ask to work with you. This is a GOLDEN Opportunity! Imagine you received a deal from one of your agents, and the

OTHER AGENT works in a closed office you always wanted to get in to!! **This is your chance, don't blow it!!** This gives you a true reason to go and make a warm stop by the Non Directing Customer's office. This is someone who has never worked with you before and happens to be in that closed office you are trying to break into. This is someone who didn't even pick you for title and now has to *privilege* to see and hear from your throughout the transaction because you are what a true professional should be doing! Your intro should go...."Hi (front desk person), my name is David Bravo Jr with_____ we met a few weeks ago, did you get the pens?? I'm glad you got them, and I have some magic pens but I will drop those off later. I'm actually here to see Joe Agent, we are working together on a new transaction"....................."Hi pleasure to meet you Mr agent, my name is David Bravo Jr with_____ and we are doing the escrow you on 5th St. First off, congratulations it looks like an amazing property. I wanted to stop by to make sure you had my business card and to let you know you can call me at any time at any point of this escrow process! I'm sure we will have a smooth escrow but is there anything I can get you today that would make your life easier? I look forward to keeping you updated throughout the escrow and will do my absolute best to insure a smooth transaction! Have a great day!". Then make sure you thank Sarah with a big smile as you leave the reception area. **THE GOLDEN SEED HAS OFFICIALLY BEEN PLANTED!**

And even if they are not there at the office when you stop by, get their card/info from the front desk and mail them a thank you card. Shoot them a thank you introduction email. JUST DO SOMETHING TO BREAK THE ICE! The agent that has never known you or didn't even chose you for the deal, now has to work with you for the next 30-45 days of escrow! This is a huge opportunity and it doesn't stop with the introduction that just happened. A week later, stop by the office again and hand drop off a prelim or escrow instructions and say "Hi Mr. Agent, just wanted to let you know I have reviewed this file (prelim/escrow instructions/termite report/etc) and I didn't see why thing to be of major concern, just a couple of easements. Here is a copy just in case you haven't received one from escrow yet. By the way, I noticed you have a listing on Beverly Dr. {because you are researching your targets) Any offers yet? I'm sure it will sell soon, it's really a beautiful property and I love the yard! Have a great day and let me know how I can make your life easier". <u>Now, in order for you to have even asked about their own listing, you need to do your research!</u> **Win the battle before it's even fought!** I guarantee you their own rep doesn't even know their own client inventory. In between this stop and the upcoming stops before closing this specific deal, this is your chance to send some value over email or text, like an emailed flyer over ways to hold title for their customer. Or maybe a stop by the office again with a call to let them know your have the building records to the property for the buyer. Make the stops and contact as many times as possible with items of value! **This is your opportunity!** Seize it and get a new customer! By closing time, you should know exactly when it the closing is set up to send a call out "Hey Mr. Joe Agent just wanted to give you a heads up we are closing your deal tomorrow and I'm personally going to take care of the recording. By the way, I recommend you order the prelim early for the short sale listing you have on Texas Dr., it's for your protection (More later)! Would you like me to place the request?" It's that simple! Even after recording the file, imagine you stop by the customers office one last time to say "Hey Mr. Agent just want to personally thank you again for allowing me to be of service. I want to bring you this certified copy of the deed to our deal we just closed to pass on to your buyer so they can use it for their utilities etc, instead of them waiting it to be mailed." And if your state regulations allow, give them a little closing gift. **THIS IS NDC** and this is how you win over a new agent! In addition to servicing your own customer who fought for you to get the deal, you've just made a huge impression on a completely new customer you didn't even know 30 days prior. Add them to your database, they should be yours!

Now how hard was that?!?! I guarantee more times than not, you just eclipsed whatever joke service they were receiving by their rep and you now just won over a customer to a closed office! Remember, all it takes is one! The hardest part is done and you are now a proven asset to any agent that wasn't using you! Now that you have outshined the competition and acquired the new agent, all you have to do now is continue to visit the new agent you have and slowly win over whoever is sitting next to them. There is no excuse for one NOT to turn into two, if you are doing your job efficiently and effectively. I guarantee if you continue to offer unrivaled service you can turn one customer into 5, within a month if you work hard enough. How do you turn one agent in two or five? Every single time you stop by your new customer (in a closed office) to service them, you need to give someone else your business card and say " **Pleasure to meet you Joe Superstar, I work with (the new agent you just got) and let me know how I can make your life easier!**" We are going to Ping and Drip (more later), and parlay every one customer until you are working with 5. Title or escrow reps who have exclusive rights to a closed office will NEVER work as hard as you will because their business is handed over to them. It's your time to shine now! <u>Win them over one by one, but your toughest part has already been conquered of acquiring the first agent because of using NDC warm prospecting!</u> <u>THE FIRST AGENT HAS BEEN AQUIRED AND THAT'S ALL YOU NEED BECAUSE NOW YOU HAVE A PURPOSE TO STOP BY AND COINCIDENTIALLY MEET MORE AGENTS, **IT'S OVER**.</u>

Just to be clear if you are new in the business or are in need of MORE customers (which YOU are), you need to use NDC every single time you get a deal with every single agent (not only with agents in closed offices). Every single file you open provides a launching pad to easily acquire another customer which you never had before! I guarantee 99 out of 100 reps do not do this! And if they do it, they do not do it consistently.

If you want more customers in your pool to draw from, you need to do this! <u>The main objective of winning over agents one by one in a closed office is to get to a point where the secretary knows you already work with ten agents in the office and they don't even stop you at the door any more.</u> You are allowed to walk in the office and then you start treating it like an Open Office. Remember to worship and win over the front desk, they will either let you in with a smile or shut you down and turn you in to their managers. Do yourself a favor and SMOOOOOZE them! The rest is all you!

Step up and outshine the competition with smart tactical HARD WORK! To attack every closed office this way. You need to break into closed office because this is where the gold lies, this is where the top agents to any areas are insulated.

Be Relentless!!!

Chapter 7 Start at

"0"

According to Webster's, definition of 0 is absence of all quantity. Every day you wake up, you need to start at zero. You need to have zero quantity every morning. The reason why you are starting at zero is because that's where you are, you've done nothing today. I don't care what you did yesterday. <u>I don't care is yesterday was the best day of your career or worst, today the only day that matters.</u> I don't care if you have been working with some big investor who is going to make it big and give you all their deals tomorrow. Today is the day, the only day! You are officially at zero when your alarm goes off. Today you are not the best rep in the company, today you do not work with top producers, today has begun and you are an unrealized gain of the stock market. The only way you can cash it out, is if you open an order today! Don't you dare go home with a goose egg, push yourself today to have one good day. Make it the best day of your life! Then when tomorrow comes, repeat your success! Then have the best week of your career, turning into the best month, turning into the best year, turning you into an unstoppable sales force to be recognized with awards and an abundant life......all because today you started at 0 and went out with a purpose to success. Be hungry and do not go home unless you're full! Every day, start at "0", this was huge for my mindset and approach every morning.

Chapter 8   Stay in your

Lane!

This chapter is so vital if you are new (or newer) to the business. One of the best opportunities we have to take advantage of is the ability to control how we (a newer rep) set out in capturing new business. To this, I say STAY IN YOUR LANE! Stay in your area as close and tight as possible! The reason why we want to keep our areas or territories as tight as possible is to maximize and concentrate our exposure. **There is a huge difference between a shotgun blast and a sniper shot.** The sniper is completely focused of their target while the shotgun is trying to capture anything it can hit wasting 99 percent of their ability to fire. Now I am aware that territories and differ greatly because of populations or demographic geographies. At the end of the day you need to maximize the amount of stops or calls you make on any given day. Do not spend more hours in the car than you do in from of customers.

One of the main supporting evidence I have to push you to stay tight is your own customers. Think about it, if you have an agent that leaves their office, they don't travel across the county for a new location, they stay close by to their farm and past customers. Our agents will stay in the pockets and so should you, maximize your exposure in a tight pocket first them expand conservatively. Do not be a *jack of all/king on none*, focus you skills and dominate! Your farm will grow organically but you need to swarm an area first. Do yourself a favor....and Stay in your Lane!

Before the

Deal

One of the most important sales strategies is learning how to lock in the title before the escrow is even opened. The main area you need to be focused on before attempting this strategy is what kind of customers and even market you are dealing with. In other words, <u>don't try this in a weak market and definitely don't try this if you are working with C or less customers. And do not try this with brand new prospects you have never worked with before, you haven't earned the right!</u> You will look like a buffoon and sabotage your closing ratios! As long as you have a stable to strong market AND you are dealing with A or B customers.....lock in their deals early! So How do we do this?

These opportunities are available every day while you are either tracking the market with a system that notifies you of new listings OR you are tracking the new inventory through the MLS. Upon one of your current customers obtaining a new listing, you have to order the preliminary title report now (or escrow instructions/any report you can attach their name to)! Your script should be something like "Hey Mr. Realtor, and congrats of your new listing on Maple. Looks like a great property that should sell quickly. As a value added service, since I know you open escrow on everything you list, I'm going to order the prelim now to make sure we don't have any surprises before we even get to escrow. Is that Ok with you? Great, what escrow officer will you be using, I will notify them as well." **Done Deal.** This strategy is huge especially when the agent you're working with does not give you every deal or loyalty may be in question. This strategy only works in seller directing areas but you need to always thing how can you lock in these deals! You can also use this strategy if you are a rep outside of title. It doesn't matter what service you provide for them, as long as you give them something that make them perceive they have committed to giving you that deal.

The ability to lock in a deal also alleviates a few potential challenges ahead. My favorite way to use this strategy was when dealing with short sale and it was actually true. "Mr. Agent, congrats on your new listing on Maple. Noticed it was a short sale, lets order the prelim now to make sure a 50k judgment doesn't blow up in our face." So by ordering the info first**, you really are protecting them**. You are also saving yourself from a call immediately after opening escrow that is the customer demanding the prelim the same day because it's a rush file. And you are finally allowing yourself to get your mind off wondering whether you going to get that deal or not, and begin focusing on the next one. <u>This is how you run numbers; this is how you will be able to beat your competition</u>! This is the difference between catching sales and grabbing sales. It's not being aggressive because you're already working with them and you are providing them a service superior.

Another angle I would use in the past to capture the deal before it even got to escrow was with a special property profile or CMA which agents would love to order. Now this CMA was better than the others because it was color and had more bells and whistles, and was even bound. The reason why I used a special product like this was because it was ordered for the end customer as well, buyer or seller. So it let me know a deal was about to happen before it even happened. It let me know an agent was about to get a listing because they used my presentation to get it! You are the king/queen of your kingdom, start controlling you destiny and create your own luck! Start thinking outside of the box in whatever market you are in, how can I lock in these deals quicker and with more effectiveness? And then your competition will all be saying, "Aw shucks, that Sally Title Rep. is so lucky! She just got a 3 million dollar deal from a customer that uses both of us......why does she always get the good ones?"

Chapter 10 Qualify the

Customer

Early in my career, I would get sucked into spending hours with a potential customer that did a whopping one deal per quarter! This was MY FAULT (and yours) because we didn't do our research! Even now as a sales manager, I see many reps spinning their wheels just to get that one deal from a C customer. You must qualify every single prospect you are targeting, and even working with. Now I believe in helping and my core foundation is service based, but I also am not here to spend half a day working with someone who is going to do a mail out for their first escrow of the year......unfortunately it's June!!

I know this is really a chapter that is going to take you back to the scheduling chapter but I cannot stress this enough. Where the mind flows is where the energy goes so you need to constantly remind yourself " if I'm going to continue to work with BC players, that's all I will ever be myself. The A players work with the A player, and solve the A problems making the A money!

For every hour you spend with a C customer, you are taking away from prospecting the A and B customers. Take care of your Cs, but **do not kill your day**. And you might be saying "But some Cs turn into As!" Well that's great, when they are a B treat them accordingly, and even better when they are an A treat them like gold. Our job as a sales rep is not to spoon feed an agent to be a success. I believe we can help and share knowledge to the masses, but not spend a day with a newbie showing them how to farm or cold call for the first time because you have just wasted your day. If you are that passionate about teaching new agents how to succeed in the business or real estate and you have mediocre title numbers, maybe you should just be an agent yourself! I'm not saying ignore C clients, I am saying protect you time and use it to its most goal orientated efficient manner. I can honestly go on and on about this but just do me a huge favor, qualify the customer!

Chapter 11 Shock and

Awe

If you get a chance google a **Success Magazine article on Shock and Awe** (a realtor strategy to get listings), it was an incredible article and I wondered how can I make the biggest impression on an A customer I was going to get. After soft selling and pinging someone long enough, you will develop enough skill to reach out once in a while and ask for the business in a way you are not being a grease ball trying to get a commission.

We are service based and in our efforts to provide the best service possible, once in a while it is our duty to go waaaay above and beyond our duty. Our job is to be the ABSOLUTE best rep we can be, until we finally reach a professionalism that is in our veins.

When your confidence builds over time on how you can perform on a per deal basis, you almost want to show off. So there was this one top producing customer I had been calling on for a couple of months. Although he was in a small office, he was actually the top agent of the city he worked. So after multiple stops over a couple of months I told myself "I know I can win this guy over if I just had one opportunity" so I asked for it. I talked to his processor on day and I asked for the opportunity to show what I can do. I told her <u>"So here's the deal Ms Processor, I'm sure you can verify I'm a hard worker based upon seeing me the last few months. But what you don't know is why I can serve you better than ANY other rep, even better than the one you are using. What I would like to do is have the opportunity to work on one deal for you. I don't want any other deals, I just want one to show you what I can do and perform. You</u>

can even give your lowest sales priced hard deal! I don't care, I just want to work with you!" She said "Ok that's fine, here's one on Opportunity street" I immediately said thank you and it was my time to blow her socks off! This was my moment!

I took the information and let her know I would notify escrow as well. I called the escrow officer immediately and placed the order for a prelim. I called my production manager immediately and asked for a huge favor for a 911 rush on a prelim. I then immediately drove to the city hall where the property was located to the building and safety department and proceeded to acquire every building record available on the property. By the end of the day, the prelim was not only completed but I hand delivered the copies of building records on the property. By the next day I already had a farm package with labels delivered in the morning and I reviewed the prelim so I was able to call the processor with news there were no red flags against the property. I also had the broker and processor set up on all of our systems and even had my customer service manager call them to introduce themselves for future requests. The following week, I made it a point to let the agent know

I was going to **personally** handle the recording of the deeds when the deal was going to close. The deal closed shortly after via my special recording and it was a <u>done deal</u>. To add a little frosting on the cake, I brought a copy of the deed to the NDC and 2 thank you cards went out to both agents, but more importantly the damage was done. After 30 days of committing to providing the absolute best service in the industry, it was over…**The customer was mine forever.**

Immediately after closing, I called the agent directly and said thank you for the opportunity (for the 5th time) and reiterated the services is was able to provide. I let him know any and all of these services were at his fingertips by getting ahold of me. His previous rep never did anything for him, just bought him donuts once in a while. I was now an asset to his team and was at his disposal for any future requests. Now let's be clear, I did not do this for every transaction he opened with me, but I will prove I can do it on the first one with this A player. I also didn't do this for every customer I acquired because I didn't have the time. **This was a Top Producer and I had one shot to give it all I got. I proved myself to him**

with working my butt off for one deal. Remember, this wasn't about 1 deal, this was about locking in a lifelong customer and embarrassing whomever they were previously using! Are you doing the same or just saying thanks for the order and dropping off a scratchpad.....big difference! Every market is different but when you have a golden opportunity to work with a top agent, do EVERYTHING possible to show them what they have been missing out on all this time! Everything! This is what separate the big dawgs dominating the block from the barking puppies in the window. You need to carpe the freaking diem!

Shop

One of the most advanced strategies of being a top affiliate is evolving to become the ultimate source of real estate. As you master your craft at title/escrow etc, you must engulf yourself in associating with other top notch professionals. In addition to knowing all the top agents of your area, <u>you must also know all the other top recommendations to guide your customers to success.</u>

You need to be able to send your customer to a top attorney, marketing company, website company, or even emergency lender at any given time without blinking. Just to clarify, by "lender" I'm referring to a possible hard money lender to step in a close a 911 deal, not a regular lender. Disclaimer.....under no circumstances should you ever marry yourself to a lender by setting up exclusive deals to exchange customers or ever go on the field together, the only thing you are going to do is commit fiscal suicide to your other potential lender customers. **Stay neutral at all times!** Why affiliate yourself to just one lender when you can work with 50 lenders!?! Ok back to One Stop Shop.

I was able to pride myself by knowing every best service provider in real estate. The key of this advanced strategy is you better be damn sure you know this referral and they truly are the best because your butt is on the line. If an agent asked me for a hard money lender I gave him 2 options. If he needed a probate attorney, I worked with one of the best in the area and I trusted them whole heartedly. If the agent was looking to do mail out, I not only know 2 different local company but I also could refer them to

2 different websites as well. I know pricing and what worked best with other top agents. If an agent wanted to create a broker website, I had a couple of companies. If an agent needed a mobile notary, here's 3. And if a broker or manager needed a speaker for an upcoming meeting, it was my duty to give them a list of my motivational speaker contacts, marketing trainers, and technology trainers at the drop of a dime. I had a speaker or service provider for ever need necessary, and you need to establish a list for yourself as well! Best question I loved to ask a client was "In the next 6 months, where and how do you want to grow your business (web/marketing etc)?" then….**fulfill their needs**! Your answer should NEVER be "Hmmm, you need a probate attorney? I'm not sure maybe check the phone book." Shame on you if you ever said this! My answer way "Absolutely Margaret, feel free to call John G. at_____. He's the best, I know him well and let him know I referred you to him so he takes good care of you" or many times I'd actually make the first intro call for the customer! By the way, make sure you follow up on every referral every time.

One of the biggest reasons I would love to refer business to other sources because **referrals would come back to me tenfold.** This is how reciprocating referrals occur! I can't tell you how much business I got referred back to me. I would even get the heads up, on up and coming clients that were starting to take off. Either way, the most important message is I was the first to know of any and all important opportunities! Again you should check your local and state regulations to do this legally and effectively. And by the way, don't you sare pay for these services you refer them to, just give them the best referral possible. There are so many laws now that handcuff our industry. Start creating a list and relationships with the top people in any auxiliary real estate industry that your agents ask for. You should be the One Stop Shop!

Chapter 13 Ping and

Drip

This is one of my favorite chapters to write on, because it allows technology and to work for you! The best recommendation I can give to ANY business person is to **create a database**! You need to spend the time, and even it's just excel, start inputting your customers into something! They even have plenty of apps that will actually auto populate a business card scan into your contacts (like Card Munch). Stop being lazy and commit to this! I don't care if you are a 20 year veteran or a new hire, you need to start today!

Getting business cards one by one can be a challenge to build up your database so I recommend again getting involved with the front desk person to an office and even board of realtors. Many times the front desk person will already have a completely filled out roster than you can have emailed to you for importing.

(If you don't know some of this technology talk we're going to cover, don't worry.....pay someone to help or call up your twelve year old nephew). Many board of realtors already have databases like these already created, the key is to <u>make sure they have cell numbers and emails</u>. Another helpful tool is to even go out and buy an actual database online. There are many companies who will actually gather all this info for you and create a downloadable list for you for a fee. Google "Real Estate Lists" or "Real Estate Email Databases" and you will find them. It will be the best $100 you will ever spend in your life! And lastly if you are lucky enough to have a market tracker system like MTA or REA, you can actually download a list straight from this. What is even cooler is the fact that you can customize the list you are looking to get more top customer info from. Be as specific as possible when it comes to pulling the data. If you were in a "seller choose" services county, you should download the top 200 listing agents in your area. If you are home warranty or termite rep, download the top 200 selling agents. **No excuses, start your database today!**

At my peak of being a rep, I had 500 actual customers but I had 1200 in my database including the agents I still wanted to acquire.

Once you have a solid list to build on, now it's time to start dripping. The first step of sending out a drip campaign is keep the info either educational of beneficial for an agent to read! Definitely don't send forwarded inspirational messages or anything that is begging the customer to unsubscribe to you! The first time I text blasted an inspirational quote, no one responded and I realized "Wow, that was really lame" but I'm coachable and I pay attention to the responses I get. Don't get me started either on the stuff real estate affiliates post on Facebook! I loved sending out market sales trends, changes in laws, or potentially some info on title the customers can benefit from. FYI, market sales trends were hands down the best to send out because every agent loves to read what the market is doing and you're providing VALUE. When you start email dripping, you will also find many systems to do it for you like Constant Contact or Mail Chimp. The challenge with these auto drip systems is that most of them will email blast for you in the middle of the night and your customers know you are actually sending it to them! If your system doesn't let you select the time when the email goes out. then send it out on your own time. There is a cool app in the iPad and iPhone called Group Email, it has a postage stamp logo and a silhouette of 2 people.

This is the greatest app I have been able to find for blasting effectively and efficiently on your own time and with your own material. It also links directly to your email for the contacts to blast to. Check it out, you're welcome.

My other favorite thing to do is to ping. I love calling text messaging "pinging" instead of texting because it sounds cooler. I also like to say I'm "pinging" someone while simultaneously flicking my index finger.....**Ping**! I absolutely loved texting instead of email or calling many of times. One of my all-time favorite things to do was to ping my customers congrats on new listings. Due to the fact I was always tracking the new listings (as covered in an earlier chapter), I always had a reason to Ping. This text was short and simple "Congrats on your new listing on Maple". That's it! The seed has been planted and your job is done when they say "thank you!" I did this every day, religiously Title Bible style. A basic message like "Congrats……" resonates with your customers because it says *I know your business, I'm happy for you, and I thank you for your future business in advance.*

In addition to pinging the customers I worked with, I especially pinged customers I didn't know or ever worked with! And the text read the same "Congrats on your new listing on Main St." Many times I wouldn't even put my name on the text so the agent would normally reply "Thanks, who is this" at which I would get into it..... "I'm David Bravo Jr with _____ Title, just wanted to say congrats! Looks like a nice property and should sell fast" if the texting continued, so did I but if the texting stopped from the customer I didn't care because I just planted a seed and the next time I saw them in person I just had a reason to walk up and say hello! Once again, the next time I see them its a much more warmer reception. **PLANT SEEDS EVERYTHING SINGLE DAY!**

And lastly, my best gold nugget I can give you is personalized text blasting. One the reason again why I like text blasting instead of emailing is because everyone always has their cell phone with them and not everyone gets their emails on their cell. So here we go.......when I first started text blasting my response rate from customers was mediocre at best to my general "Hope you have a great holiday weekend!" the problem was after a while, my clients started getting these generic messages and started realizing they were just part of my blast! There is nothing like a personal text and so we enter the game of auto populated texts. I found out there were apps for this also! For Droid users download TextBlast and for Apple users download TextMachine or Smurge (and there are plenty more now available).

Once again, you're welcome. What this app does is allow you to select multiple contacts and send them a text blast. The best part of these apps is the ability to merge the person's name into the text itself. Kind of tough to explain but instead of sending a message that reads "Happy New Year, wishing you a great 2014!" a TextMachine/Smurge/TextBlast message can read "Happy New Year Mark, wishing you a great 2014!", next one would read "Happy New Year John" etc....so basically the app charges the name of Mark to John to whom the message is being sent to, and it does it automatically for you! This was HUGE for me! I would send out TextMachine blasts out on a Friday that read "Have a great weekend (auto name), let me know if you need anything emailed before the end of the day or want anything on your desk first thing Monday morning!" <u>So the customer actually thinks I am sending them a personalized message when they are one of 300 agents receiving the same message.</u> There are so many options to use this app for; I could probably write a book on it by itself! Another one of my favorite text blasts was on Monday morning " Hey (auto name) have a great week! Let me know how I can make your life easier!" And every major holiday, I would send out something special like " Happy New Year (John), just want to sincerely wish you the best year possible and I am grateful for being a part of your team!" Imagine that personalized message going to 200 or even 500 of your customers!!

My response rate on generic text blasts was less than 10 percent, auto populated texts were 95 percent because the person's name was in the text itself. Yes 95%! When you download the app, try it on a couple of friends or family so you could see how it works. Then let the mass pinging begin! In addition to once a month email blast, <u>you should be text blasting another once a month toward the middle of the month and special holidays</u>. Space the blasting out from each other so you don't overdo it and make sure you don't blast them so much you are just annoying! **Commit to doing this and I guarantee your business will grow EXPONENTIALLY!**

Chapter 14 Voice

Command

Perfect segway into another favorite trick no one is using..... Sly Broadcast. I stumbled onto Sly Broadcast earlier last year 2015. I wasn't too sure about the concept and then I started realizing the full potential as I tried it for the first time. First off what is Sly Broadcast? Sly Broadcast is an additional service added to Sly Dial. Sly Dial allows you to leave a voicemail for a person, without actually having to call them. It bypasses there ringing of their phone on their side and goes directly to the voicemail. The person will get a voice mail alert and see your missed call but will never actually have their phone ring. This is a great tool when used properly if you don't want to speak with a customer directly, or maybe even your spouse! Now, back to Sly Broadcast.

Sly Broadcast takes the same concept and allows you to do it to the masses. I tested this out first with my sales team and it worked flawlessly. You basically can create one audio file (it will become your voicemail), take that file........ and then send it out to as many people as you like. So my voicemail went like this, "Hey everyone its David Bravo Jr, just want to wish you a fantastic day and a fantastic month! The same message then went out to 22 reps with one click.

Now back to the use of dealing with customers. Imagine you can take a single voice mail, and distribute it to the top 500 realtors in the market. Imagine a voicemail something like this, "Hey I'm glad you got your voicemail, this is David Bravo Jr! I just was just thinking about you and wanted to wish you

Happy Thanksgiving. Let me know if there's anything I can email you or fax you before the weekend. Once again as always have a great extended weekend and I'll see you soon. **Imagine that voicemail going out to five hundred Realtors!** The beauty and secret to all of this is the fact that the people you left the voicemail for have no idea you're using Sly Broadcast to send it out. They think you actually called them, and they missed your call, and you left them a voicemail individually. This is a huge way to get out to the masses with very little effort. If I was a sales rep today I would use this at least once a month. It may be just to wish everyone a great holiday or it may be to announce a new product that we have with our company. Either way this is a way to get out to the masses. Now the secret is this, you have to leave a voicemail that sounds natural and that sounds that you actually left it for someone without sounding like a automated robot. So remember to use phrases like "Hey I'm glad I got your voicemail, this is Bravo Jr. Just wanted to leave you a quick message that I have a new tool in title that I think you would absolutely love. Shoot me a text when you get a chance for more details." **I would expect no less than a couple**

hundred text messages or responses about that tool! My final advice is be prepared. Be prepared to receive as many messages out to people as you left. Make sure you're in a place where you can literally sit down and just be on your phone returning all these messages. And once again keep the secret!! Make sure that no given point you tell your customers that you're using a system like Sly Broadcast! You're welcome again.

Chapter 15 Take a picture,

it'll last longer

This will be the shortest chapter in the book, and I don't care. Get a picture and get a good picture please! Do me a favor and spend the money even if your company doesn't reimburse you and invest in yourself....please! This is it, this is what the customers see on your business card, email promo, or even social media. Ask yourself, how many people look at my Facebook or LinkedIn? How many business cards do I hand out each year? Hew many promo flyers do I hand out? How many emails do I send each year? This is a no brainer! Just put on the best outfit you have a get a darn professional picture people will gravitate to and want to work with. Smile big, and don't try to looks cocky or sexy...just be you! That's what your customers want! Authenticity! It's the most used advertising you can invest in and one of the most embarrassingly used as well. Believe me, I've seen atrocious business photos and its alarming! Get a pic! Check out addthewow.com, Mario is *in my opinion* the best photographer on the planet for professional photos. If he is too far from you, find someone closer and show them this is what you're going for. Pay $200 every 3 years, I guarantee it is worth your money and time for a day!

Be Different

One of my favorite things to do was to brainstorm on different ideas of how I can differentiate myself from my lesser foe competitors. So this chapter brings me to promo branding. I cannot take credit for my mindset on this one. <u>When I got into title at 18 years old I was able to witness the best title rep in the world, my father David Bravo Sr.</u> I got to see him in action by going on the field with him as early as 6 years old spending summer handing out blow pops and calling customer service to order a profile. One of the coolest thing I was able to see early on was how my father <u>separated himself from the competition</u>. First off, his special edition business cards contained his baby picture which was cool and different. Now it wasn't an actual infant picture, but it still was a picture taken when he was about 4 years old. He had a silly grin on his face as a young boy, and it was a HUGE marketing technique on the field. He was being different and the customers loved it and remembered him for it. I could remember countless times when he'd meet a new customer they would say "Oh so you're Bravo, I have seen your baby pictures everywhere but I've never known what you actually looked like". Customers would know and remember him before he'd even call on their office. Who doesn't like baby pictures?

The 2nd trademark I saw early on from my father was wearing Disney or Looney Town neck ties. Again he was able to separate himself from the crowd because everyone (and their mothers) loved his ties. Don't misunderstand this tactic, he always was very well dressed. He just happened to incorporate something memorable in his outfit. He was always able to bring a smile to the customers' faces because his ties were so animated, literally. His current technique used is wearing some of the coolest fedoras the fashion industry can offer. It's quite the dapper look!

When I came into title in 1999, I was quick to jump in the baby picture bandwagon. Worked like a charm! As my career evolved, I would try to add my own spin to marketing. I remember early in my career, I would put riddles on my promotional flyers that my clients would love. Then I would tie the riddle into giving them a reason to call me. "Call me in order to get the answer to this brain buster"

Later on in my career, I started recalling branding myself with my trademark catchphrase HOW CAN I MAKE YOUR LIFE EASIER? I created a whole marketing campaign around something I would ask my customer's every day! I created mouse pads with my own version of an Easy Button on it. I put HOW CAN I MAKE YOUR LIFE EASIER? on the back of my business cards. I'd love the leave these business cards on desks or phone with just that phrase showing because everyone has to turn it over and smile. Besides that campaign, one of my favorite marketing ideas came from some custom pens I made. I created some pens the read on the side Bravo Jr's Magic Pen. Every single time I would give this pen away I would say "Hi Ms Realtor, I have a special gift for you today. I have imported these pens from a land far far away and these pens are magic! (smile) So here's why they are so special..... **You know how your real estate sale contracts list what title company will be insuring this transaction. When you get to this part of the contract, this pen will magically start writing Bravo Jr! I swear!** I dare you to try it today!" Huge hit for me and also gave me major follow up like "Did you try the pen yet?" or "Haven't seen a deal from you, maybe you got a faulty pen, **here's a new one!**" My days were always fun because I kept marketing fresh and fun. There are so many great ideas online now, you just have to put them into action! Be different, and incorporate it into your marketing ASAP! This is where your personality should really shine. If you lack in the fun department, go to a local marketing company and ask them for ideas. Even if you have to invest in hiring a professional, make the investment!

Chapter 17 Bad days and

Good Days

I cannot stress enough how important it is to be on your game, <u>every single day</u>! There cannot be a day in which you go to an office and your customer should **EVER** have a reason to ask you "Are you feeling well?" or "Long day?" If you are running at an extremely high production level, and running right through your projected goals, there is going to be a time where you are just in a funk and having a bad day. This is OK!! Maybe you are going through personal challenges, could be anything, maybe you are having a challenging time with your children or spouse. Maybe you just spilled your morning coffee on your white shirt, a rock hit your windshield, and you got a parking ticket all before 10am. Maybe you are just having BAD DAY. It's OK!!

Please do yourself, and your customers, a favor and go home. Get home as soon as possible, change your clothes, and call it a day. I would rather you go home and regroup your mind before seeing another customer. Customers see and notice everything and should not see you in a bad mood or bent out of shape because you are having a tough day. Even if you have to take two days off, do it! Come back to work reenergized and with a clear mindset to bring you're A Game. There is no such thing as a Bad Day Game, or even a Tired Game. **The ONLY game your customer needs to be exposed to is you're A Game, no exceptions**. If you are not at the highest mindset level possible, you're worthless. No one wants to be around Debbie Downer! In addition to being a sad little puppy dog no one wants to be around, you also run the risk of a customer pushing you to the limit. The very last thing you would ever want to do in this world is blow up on a customer because you had other things go sour in your day. Never ever take your frustrations out on anyone on your team or especially a customer. Bite your tongue and pass it to someone you can trust who could help you for the day. Just be ready to regroup, and step your game up tomorrow!

Now let's talk about the Good Days, you need to promise me you are going to soak these days up for all they are worth. Some days you will have good opening or closing day, maybe you just got a new customer, or maybe just you woke up feeling GOOD! Either way, you need to push this day until the sun goes down, and then make one more stop! I promise your customers feed off your good vibes and there is nothing better in the world than to be able to work with a giant ray of sunshine. You're exuding success and you need to share it with the world! I once lived in Las Vegas for a whole 7 months of my life (too much for a 22 year old with money to handle) and I read this book on Blackjack called Master the Flow. It was basically a book about the flows of a blackjack deck and sometimes you will get a hot deck that you just need to ride all the way to the bank! It doesn't matter what cards are coming out, you are either going to pull 20 or 21 or the dealer is going to bust. The book describes how you need to increase your bets and put you money in the middle until things slow down. Same thing with business, some days you are going to be unstoppable out there, you need to make sure these days last as long as possible! Master that Flow! Get in front of as many people as possible; even skip lunch if you have to! Let that positive energy poor out of you like a walking lottery winner because the truth is, you did win the lottery! **This is the greatest**

business on the world and you should act accordingly! Celebrate today with joy and love, celebrate your next deal and kiss your customers! Start today and make it a great day! Why not? Someone is going to have a great day, why not you? This also circles back to the basic fundamental of dressing great carrying over to your daily activity. I know exactly what kind of day I'm going to have just by the outfit I'm wearing. That why I weeded out all the clothes that didn't make me feel sensational! Back to the good days, be aware of them and soak them for all their worth. You'll see, the more good days you can have equate to a good month. Next thing you know it a good quarter on your way to a GREAT YEAR. Master that flow and stick with it! Have a good day!

Soft Selling

I learned early in my career that there are two very different techniques on how to "sell" or "close" people. The first mindset of hard selling is one of aggressive selling through getting a direct commitment from customers. The second mindset of soft selling is one of a subtle approach where you hope the customers observes you working for the deal and hopefully you'll get it. There is a big chasm between these two different approaches because they are polar opposites in the way the both get and keep customers. Before I explain which one I favor and why, it's imperative to know how to do both.

In my early years of title, I remember dealing with some managers in my company that insisted on asking for the deal! Having been only 18 years old, I had a big challenge with asking my 50+ year old client for their next deal. Maybe it was a lack of skill, lack of knowledge of how to do it, or purely a lack of guts but either way asking for the biz never happened. What did happen was basic and remedial showing up. I showed up, I asked anyone if they needed anything, and I smiled. I especially loved the question "How can I make your life easier?" Notice that has NOTHING to do with title! Over the next several years, I realized I never asked the business from anyone. I just continued establishing new relationships! I knew I would get business as long as I was around, and I was always available to my customers and go the extra mile when needed!

What I didn't know was I was establishing the grass roots of soft selling. I learned this from my father. The theory of, if you are always available and consistent about making your in person office visits, there is no reason why you will not eventually get business. <u>The competition is lazy and will mess up a file one day, you just need to be the Plan B for when it happens.</u> Later in my career, I took soft selling to a new level when I combined it with a **superior level of commitment.** You see when you have a well established schedule and target customer wish, all you need a ridiculous work ethic and you will get their business without even asking for it. They know why you're there, they know what you want. You don't have to make someone feel uncomfortable by asking for their next deal! You need to remember that if you take a **long term approach** to this business, it doesn't matter whether it's a month or a year, if you commit to being consistently present it will happen! <u>It's a marathon, not a sprint.</u>

While I would not usually directly ask for the deal, I still heavily relied on the **assumptive close.** After taking care of any major request from a customer, I was notorious in closing with "I'll keep an eye out for an open escrow on this one to make sure we rush your request" or "Looking forward to seeing this one opened, I know *you've* worked hard on it". Never once have I ever said "I worked hard, can I have your next transaction?" it always just felt super sleazy to me. Many times the basic congrats to their new listing is a subliminal closing technique I always used "Congrats on Maple Ave". What you're *really* telling them is "I know you have a new listing, and now you know that I know, I also will be looking out to open title!" There's no need to take a hard closing approach, it's going to come with relentless service over time.

Remember it's a marathon not a sprint and you have to have the mindset of it doesn't matter who the competition is I'm GOING TO WEAR THEM OUT!

Chapter 19 Competing with the

Competition

I would like to take this time to say thank you. Thank you to my former competing sales reps who continued to drive and push me to success. If I am lucky enough to have you read this, thank you! Now let's get back to business shall we. One of my Why's is to compete. It's tough to explain but I love to battle against the best. Sometimes is wasn't even about the deal any more, it was just about winning and defeating my competitors. **Kobe, Jordan, Tyson, and Vince Lombardi style.....win, win, win**. So before we get to the fun stuff, let's start from the beginning.

To be clear, one of the most important recommendations I can give you is be absolutely respectable to every competitor your meet and even shake their hands and acknowledge when possible. There is no place in the business world for dirty competition of throwing away business cards or gossiping about another person. There is a place in this world for bringing your competition to their knees by outsmarting and outworking them. The way you do this is with mindset, mindset, and mindset. When I had the privilege of competing with some of the best in the industry, I would get excited! I would get excited because I knew in my heart and soul I was going to outwork them. I knew for the new offices, I was going to win the deals every day because I had **service based strategies** that was going to make them hate me. They hated me because they knew they would have to actually work harder just to keep up. I didn't care because I knew in my heart I was going to wear them out! Some tried keeping up, but all failed over time! Anyone can work hard for a month, anyone can even work hard for 6 months. But after a while they will slow down. They will slow down because you will keep imposing your will upon them! And as they slow down their retaliation efforts, you bring it even more! Bring it like it never been brung before ☺

Current offices that were already dominated by me, I would smile at the new competition because I viewed it as a giant waste of time for them. My customers were mine and any efforts they used to pursue them would leave themselves taking time away from the other accounts they would get business from. This is where knowing your competition is key. If you know your competitors best customers, this is a silver platter opportunity to return the favor and visit their offices and <u>light em up like a Christmas tree!</u> Sometimes you can do this just for fun and you will see them never go to your offices ever again, there is another reason why you need to know your completion is to learn from them! One of my best qualities when dealing with competition out on the field was keeping my mouth shut and my eyes and ears open. Watch and learn from your competitors, see their sales angles and pitches, and even ask top agents that use them "How did _____ earn your business?" Really learn from them, **especially the ones who are the best in your area!** There are so many core values when learning from the top that I didn't have early on. Healthy competition is so good, because it will bring out the best in YOU! You can't be the best unless you beat the best so we might as well find out right now what you're made of! One of my favorite competitors was an incredible rep on perseverance. Even though I would win a customer over, combined with his company completely blowing a deal, and he even looked like a fool by having a few cocktails to many at real estate events. This guy kept coming back for more. I absolutely LOVED this about him! I'm serious; I have nothing but respect for him because he kept coming back for more. And thank you in advance to all the sales managers who I'm now competing with. With all sincerity, I am honest and ethical. On a personal level I have nothing but best wishes to them.........but I looooove to compete and you make me take my approaches to the highest levels possible. Thank you for making me a better sales manager, every day.

Chapter 20   How much do you Value

YOURSELF?

Now that we have a clear visual potential of business and have a schedule in place, it's time to stay true to your values and stay true to gaining and keeping customers as a result of great service! I cannot stress this enough. From the wise words of one of the leading advisors of real estate, David Kellerman said it best "Our job is to GET customers, KEEP customers, and grow our market share PROFITABLY". There is no other way. There is no easy way except for answering your phone when called or return messages immediately. Take care of the requests immediately and FOLLOW UP! "Hey Mrs. Top agent, I just wanted to reach out and make sure you received that farm package yesterday. Please let me know if there is anything else I can do to make your life easier. By the way, how's the family?" Was that hard? This biggest challenge you will face on a daily basis is holding yourself accountable. Your manager isn't going to be there every day holding your hand to make sure you ordered a request. But I promise you this, numbers do not lie and you will be held accountable one way or another. So do yourself a favor and HOLD YOURSELF ACCOUNTABLE. Commit to yourself every day. From the wise words of Thomas Edison "There is NO Substitute for Hard Work". Some of the following paragraphs may strike a nerve with people! I'm passionate against certain practices but I'm not blinded to the 50 shades of title. I know there are certain necessary evils, but we can at least commit to making the first reason your customers give you business is because of the service you provide.

Do not try to buy business or discount your way to the top! All you doing is publishing to the world you are not good enough to COMPETE so you are now a cheap date (I have plenty other synonyms that I would like to use but I won't) when you buy a customer, you are begging for another customer to ask for the same, it's a slippery slope and should never be entertained. Along the same lines, do no try to provide services above and beyond what your job is. Our job is to provide honest superior service, not print postcards or flyers. Just to clarify, many states have laws against many forms of alleged kick-backs like paying for someone's printing. This was a major problem in Southern California that all the reps were doing, it was proving they are a cheap date (gosh I wish I can say something else). Do not try to discount fees on your way to success and hope you don't get outbid by another rep, because it will happen. The biggest challenge with this is you will never be known for your service or what value you bring to the agents business, the only reason they are using you is because you're the cheapest. How degrading does that sound?!? By being the cheapest not only have you marginalized your own worth, but now you have begun attracting the worst customers on this planet. The customers that will ask you repeatedly in a slimy voice "Hey can I get another discount? Or can we go a little lower on this one?" WTH? How about No! I'm not saying every once in a while we shouldn't be able to help a consumer with pricing. I am saying that if your business model is based around buying business, printing flyers, or being the cheapest, I promise you will die a slow business death and even though you may have good numbers the world know you are a fraud. Stay true to yourself, your value, and your integrity..... Do it the right way. Get customers, keep customers, and grow market share profitably by working hard and providing HONEST SUPERIOR SERVICE!

I know this real estate broker, and he opened up to me one day because he was frustrated. He told me "David, I'm really tired of working with all these lower income FHA buyers who it is a pain in the butt to get them into a home" to which I replied "How are you getting these buyers?" He said "Well, they all are coming from my ads in the Pennysaver" **Here's the lesson**, the only reason why this broker was getting horrible buyers was because that's the horrible business he was marketing for. He wasn't marketing towards million dollar listings or buyers, he was putting himself out there for the bottom or the barrel. Know your worth as a sales rep and know what kind of business you're going after. There is plenty of good business in the world, you need to find it and direct your attention to it. If you find yourself working with a bad book of business, make it a point to focus your attention on working with a better customer base. The more thoroughbreds you have in your stable, the less mules you have to tend to. You cannot do this unless you have a high value of yourself first!

Chapter 21 Gratitude

Thank You Thank You Thank You! While some reps think they really do a decent job in thanking their customers, 95% of you don't! This was an alarming experience for me when I took a step back from my business activities and looked at how I thanked my customers. I would normally thank my customers via text, email, or sometimes call BUT this isn't good enough! <u>If you want to raise your levels of success, you need to raise the level of how you thank your loyal customers who do business with you, end even customers who have never worked with you (NDC).</u> Do yourself a favor and spend time every business day you have to hand write thank you cards! This time could either be during your morning Starbucks sit or while you're waiting for lunch. You need to do this **yesterday**!

Now if you're reading this telling yourself, "I don't have time to write cards and drop them off at the post office" then pay someone to do them for you. When I was peaking as a rep, I paid someone monthly to view every single closing I had for the day, get the customer info, and mail them a printed postcard on my behalf referencing the transaction we just closed. In addition to that, I also texted, emailed, or called the client personally. Then when I saw the customer, I again said Thank You in person! Some of you aren't saying Thank You in any way, ever….shame on you! This customer has options and I promise you will lose them on day when they get a Thank You card from a rep they don't even consistently use. Flip the script now, and use this knowledge to your advantage. Back to NDC, send a Thank You card to the realtor who didn't even direct you the deal. Imagine you are an agent who just opened escrow, next thing you know there is a thank you card waiting at your office from someone you've never even met. Do you think that could have a big impact? **Do you think if you later stopped by the office you'd get a warmer reception from the agent?** YES YES and YES!

This is how you Shock and Awe someone you have never even met before. Thank them for something they didn't even do! I GUARANTEE you that agent will be saying to themselves "Wow, this rep wrote me a hand written Thank You card for a deal I didn't even send them....my rep doesn't even thank me and I've used her for 10 years". You need to thank as many people as you can in each transaction, every time! Thank the Listing Agent, Thank the Selling Agent, Thank the Lender, Thank the Escrow Officer in advance for their hard work, thank the Title Officer and production for looking out for your customer, and send a Thank You card to the non-directing customer! Send Thanks by card, call, and handshake to your directing customer! And finally if you are committed to be the very best, get rosters of everyone's birthdays and send out a card for that as well! I dare you, watch what happens to your business......

Thank You for reading and internalizing this chapter!

Chapter 22

All about that

Base!

Database, Database, Database! This will single handedly make you a player in the big leagues or a pretender on the sidelines. This will also be your biggest influencer as you take the extra steps towards regional database. I don't care what business you are in (Title doesn't even matter), this is one of our largest inadequacies of any business. Database, or lack of, is the sole reason why you are not creating some sort of residual business and ultimately predictable income.

As a sales rep, I remember doing presentations to real estate agents and taking surveys of past client production. I remember one time I was standing in front of a smaller office of about 25 agents and I asked the group. Who here has a CRM or any type of contact management system as basic as excel? Not one hand raised up! So I looked at the broker and asked "Mr. Broker, do you have a database? He shook his head no. I was floored by his response then continued my conversation but asking him how he followed up with past clients. He mentioned "Once in a while, I will pick up the phone and call someone up" I asked "How did you know who to call." He said "Sometimes I just get a file I see laying around and find their number" Before I go any further...this is a broker who was very successful and averaged 15-25 sales a year for about 15 years. I continued by asking Mr. Broker "How much of his business was repeat business?" He sheepishly responded "Maybe one deal a year." I finally did it....I asked him "In 15 years Mr. Broker, having sold over 300 homes to wonderful clients, who came back to you? How many sellers and buyers do you think bought or sold with you and never used you again?" He said "Probably 250, because most of his homes bought or sold where first time home buyers and sellers to smaller homes that people just don't stay in long term." **So there it is! If this very successful business man would have committed to creating a tiny puddle of clients, where he could one day make a pond of clients,**

then one day he would eventually accumulate a great lake of income! Why in the heck wouldn't everyone do it? The answer is they don't know how or they don't want to. My answer is I don't care if you write did down on some master list paper, make one and commit to not being lazy! 5 years from now you will start to see the benefits.

Now that brings me to title, when I became a sales manager in 2012, I turned to my team of 17 and asked "How many of you have a database?" A whopping 2 hands raised. That's when I realized, this isn't a real estate problem or a title problem, it's a business problem! Shame on all of us for not having an ability to create residual income in our business. Now you might be saying "But David, there's no such thing as residual income in our business" to which I respond YES there absolutely is! It's called FEED THE KITTY, and if you are out of sight...you're out of mind. You need to be in sight and in mind, whenever anyone considers title or considers replacing their own pretender title rep. This is how you do it, now I'm not going to go into details of how to create a beautiful database from scratch but you can start by creating one by simply asking for rosters from front desk personal of the offices you call on. Even better ask for an already done spreadsheet roster in excel and just start piling them on top of one another. Or do what I did, I got print outs of as many agents lists I could acquire and start typing. I spent a whole weekend sitting in front of a spreadsheet in the summer of 2008 and it was done. The key is to get it into a "csv" format thru excel and then you could take that baby anywhere. FIRST NAME, LAST NAME, OFFICE NAME OFFICE, ADDRESS, CELL PHONE, EMAIL IS THE MOST IMPORTANT. Just keep it basic and especially simple!

Now that we have a database, just start email dripping. Send whatever you got or whatever is available in the beginning, just send something once or twice a month! I'm not a big fan of every week but I also say it's better to do something more than you should that not do it at all! So send seasonal Happy Valentine's day pics or Happy holidays...I don't care just send it! As you perfect this skill of dripping, you can send more informative stuff with value but for now just send it! The mindset is this....maximum exposure equals maximum results. This is how your customers that are using you will always remember you when they go to write on offer or contract. And this is how the customers who are not using you will know that they have an option available to them when their current rep drops the ball. Constantly add to the database and constantly make it a part of your business. 10 years from now when you have a database of 2500 agents and loan professionals, you will thank me. You will also thank me when you have a way to contact them ALL at any given notice to announce a new territory, an award received, a new baby in the family, a new improvement in your company, or maybe even a new company you moved to! It doesn't matter, you now have a way to contact your masses. Get to it and start today. I'm proud to say almost every rep on my team now has a database and they are seeing the residuals.

Closing

I sincerely hope you have enjoyed this book. I hope it lit a fire somewhere in your soul that is smoldering in your belly tonight. I believe you have greatness in you if you are reading this. I remember once Anthony Robbins said to an audience an event by the attendees being in their chairs, the inner commitment already existed no matter what the seminar what going to cover because you took the first step of being there at the event. I feel the same way about this book. If you are reading this closing, you probably are driven enough to want to succeed. Your commitment is there, go out and start the rest of your career today with purpose and passion. Make the rest of your career, the best of your career! Always remember how blessed and lucky you are to be in the greatest business in the world! No matter what challenges you face, always remain in a state of gratitude! Godspeed and I look forward to hearing from you one day! Connect with me on Facebook, LinkedIn, leave me a review, or even send an email to BravoJr@TitleBible.com Good or bad, I'd love to hear about what your thoughts on the book are! Unless the thoughts are really really bad, then don't bother because I will unfriend you ☺ What would you have like me to dive deeper on? Is there something you'd specifically like to see in a possible Title Bible II? Most importantly, what will you do with the information received? What changes will you commit to in your business, or add to your daily activities? **I honestly do want to hear from you!** I sincerely thank you once again for taking the time to read the Title Bible, and I hope to shake your hand one day!

-David Bravo Jr

Made in the USA
Middletown, DE
02 July 2020

11118915R00066